How To Organize

A Babysitting Cooperative

and Get Some *Free* Time Away from the Kids

by Carole Terwilliger Meyers

Illustrations by Nancy Clement

CAROUSEL PRESS

*For my husband, Gene, without whose
encouragement, enthusiasm, and
editing abilities this book would never
have been completed.*

Library of Congress Catalog Card Number: 76-12660

ISBN: 0-917120-00-0 (paperbound)
ISBN: 0-917120-01-9 (hard cover)

Printed in the United States of America

Additional copies of "How to Organize a Babysitting
Cooperative" may be ordered by mail. See order
form on page 83.

CAROUSEL PRESS
P.O. Box 6061
Albany, CA 94706

ACKNOWLEDGEMENTS

I wish to express my special appreciation to:

- the members of my own babysitting co-op for putting up with my fanatical attention to detail at our business meetings;
- my husband, Gene, for his editorial help and suggestions during the painful and tedious revisions;
- and my son, David, for sleeping long naps in the afternoon and for enjoying his babysitting experiences with my fellow co-opers.

And my thanks to the following people who took time from their busy lives to help me gather my research materials: Edith Beget, Joyce Fancher, Mrs. Robert Kahn, Adean Kane, Joanne Levy, Diane Lohman, Liz Ojakian, Carole O'Neil, Elaine Perry, Sue Prior, Jean Reed, Adair Small, Michelle Stone, Marcia Varnau, and Jacqueline Vittori. Thanks, too, to Jerry Harris who helped with some of the typing. And last but not least I want to thank Dick Ellington, whose expertise at typesetting and layout is obvious throughout this book.

TABLE OF CONTENTS

INTRODUCTION

This book is intended primarily as a guide for parents interested in setting up a babysitting cooperative, or *co-op*. Much of the material included will also prove useful to co-ops which are already in operation and may help to make them run more smoothly. Established co-ops will find this book especially helpful in solving some of the problems which invariably arise and in streamlining and clarifying their existing rules and bookkeeping procedures.

Throughout this book reference is made primarily to mothers because, realistically, they are the ones who usually wind up operating a co-op and doing the requisite babysitting. But of course interested fathers are encouraged to play an active role in a co-op too. And in these liberated times when the traditional roles of husband and wife are often being exchanged, and single-parent families are becoming more common, one can expect to see a growing number of "house husbands" becoming involved in babysitting co-ops. They, too, need to get away from their chores and children occasionally and this need will sometimes arise when the woman of the house is away from home and unavailable to assist!

1

In these liberated times when the traditional roles of husband and wife are often being exchanged, and single-parent families are becoming more common, one can expect to see a growing number of "house husbands" becoming involved in babysitting co-ops.

CHAPTER I

WHAT IS A BABYSITTING COOPERATIVE?

A babysitting cooperative is a group of parents who exchange babysitting services with one another. The babysitting takes place in the members' homes, and no money is exchanged. Co-ops vary in size from an intimate group with as few as three or four families to the impersonal size of over two hundred. Any size can be workable, but a group of about fifteen to twenty seems to be the most expedient. Some co-ops are designed to function for day, night, or weekend use only, although the majority offer babysitting at *any* time.

Published data indicate that babysitting co-ops have been around for about twenty years. They appear to be an outgrowth of World War II, when parents had to cope with the baby boom. At that time many young families found themselves with small children and living in the new housing developments offering G.I. loans. Teenagers were scarce in these developments, and money was tight. I would venture that the first babysitting co-op was created by a desperate and resourceful mother. Since then the idea has been passed on basically by word of mouth.

In some areas co-ops are referred to as *babysitting exchanges, pools,* and *clubs.* It isn't hard to see why some co-ops consider themselves to be clubs. Often co-ops become an essential, interesting, and rewarding part of the members' lives.

After several years of interaction, strong bonds often form between participants, lasting friendships develop, and quite often the co-op evolves into a closely-knit social group. This is especially true of the smaller co-ops.

Some co-ops use the club analogy to be very selective in choosing new members, taking care to form a homogeneous and compatible group. Although ideally membership in a co-op should be open to anyone willing to live by the rules, in actual practice most co-ops limit membership in various ways in order to achieve a congenial and convenient group. Some groups find it more expedient to select members with similar values and interests or to restrict membership to a certain area or neighborhood. Each co-op ultimately decides for itself what method of selecting new members will best meet with its particular needs.

CHAPTER II

REASONS TO FORM OR JOIN
A BABYSITTING COOPERATIVE

It is to be expected that different people may have different reasons for joining a babysitting co-op. These are the more common ones.

Concern over the quality of care an infant receives.

With the birth of their first child, parents often find themselves feeling that they are the only people who can properly care for their baby. Most new parents feel more comfortable if their newborn is left with grandparents or relatives whom they know have successfully raised a number of their own children. If they find themselves in the very common situation of being geographically (or emotionally) distant from their relatives, they usually also find themselves in the situation of having no one to turn to for babysitting. Most parents would feel more comfortable in this situation if they could leave their infant with another mother. However, they often dislike asking friends or neighbors to help out because at this stage watching a baby can be a bit of work. And most new parents feel uneasy leaving their newborn with a stranger from an agency or with a teenager who may be inexperienced in dealing with possible emergencies.

In a co-op no one is inconvenienced (the sitter agrees to sit only if it is convenient for her and in exchange for the return service), the sitters are experienced with infants and children (they all have their own), and the parents know their sitters more than casually (co-ops offer many opportunities for members to get to know each other). Co-op parents have peace of mind that their child will be treated with the same consideration that the sitter gives her own children and that if an emergency situation occurs, another person with a developed parental instinct will be in charge.

Unavailability of daytime sitters.

Some parents may be able to get a local teenager or even a relative to watch their children at night, but during the day most pay sitters are at school and most free ones are at their jobs. When a child is very young, the parents don't have the option of playgroups or nursery schools, and most daycare centers are available only to full-time working mothers. Informal exchanges with neighbors are often not fair and can lead to irritation, misunderstandings and loss of frienship if one person is interpreted by the other as taking advantage. The option of using an agency is an expensive one since the parent winds up paying the sitter, the agency, and the sitter's carfare. The usual minimum charge is for four hours at the prevailing rate of $2–$2.50 per hour plus carfare. This cost is prohibitive for most families' budgets except on special or urgent occasions. And many mothers who can afford this cost find themselves feeling guilty for spending it on such a "frill" as daytime babysitting.

In a co-op all members will be in similar circumstances and usually would just as soon watch another child along with their own, knowing that they will have the same amount of free babysitting time open to them when they want or need it.

Lack of teenagers to hire.

Have you noticed the shrinking population of teenagers? There is a desperate shortage of teenage babysitters in my own neighborhood and of those around—some lack good judgment, some are undesirable (who wants to come home to an empty refrigerator or to find their babysitter hosting a party for the local high school?), and others are social butterflies who seem always to be too busy to babysit. The best sitters are easy to spot because they are usually busy sitting for someone else or unavailable because it is a school night.

Voilà! The co-op comes to your rescue. With a pool of people to draw from, usually at least one of them is available to help at any given time—even at the last minute!

Limited funds.

Babysitting costs can hit your budget hard. After a night out, with inflated bills for restaurants and entertainment, you may find your wallet empty when you return home. I remember the good old days when a competent babysitter like myself earned 35¢ an hour—no matter how many kids were in the family—and most families were a lot larger then. The current rate in my own neighborhood now averages $1 per hour —even for only *one* child—and I've heard of areas where it is even higher. A co-op will be a comfort to your pocketbook, as no money will be exchanged. All your babysitting will be free with the condition that you will pay back with an equal amount of your own time. It is easy to save $200-$500 per year using a co-op and not hard to save a lot more.

To figure out your own potential annual savings from using a babysitting co-op all you need do is multiply the approximate number of hours you use babysitters each year times the current hourly fee charged by local sitters. In a large city such as New York where agencies charge $2.50 per hour plus cabfare, one can quickly see the value of this type of group. In smaller towns where teenagers may charge the more reasonable rate of 75¢—$1 per hour, the savings are somewhat less—but still substantial. An average family might use a sitter two times a month for about five hours each time. At $1 per hour this would cost $10 a month or $120 a year. In New York City this would cost $300 a year. Of course, if you do join a co-op you will probably be motivated to use a sitter even more frequently to take mornings and afternoons off to shop, visit museums, attend luncheons and classes, or to pursue other such pleasurable activities unburdened by little children. So your savings may be even greater than this original estimate.

To meet people with similar interests.

Maybe you're new to your area and have not yet made new friends. Or maybe you have a new baby and find that your old friends consist almost totally of unmarried, non-parent types who don't have much in common with you any more. What a heartache it is to be with a new baby and have no one to share your joys and sorrows! You need to acquire friends with interests and problems similar to your own. A co-op will give you this opportunity and much more. My own co-op has regular picnics, pot-lucks, and parties, and most of the members belong to the same weekly playgroup. With time these shared activities help to develop warm friendships. You may find yourself teaming up with other members to can jellies, look at nursery schools, discuss child-rearing problems, teach each other new crafts, or even for a double-date! And your children will also begin gathering their own circle of little friends.

To expose a young child to different environments and to give him the opportunity to play with other children.

Do you live in a neighborhood with very few little children? (Very few teenagers, very few little children—sounds like we have already surpassed zero population growth.) Children benefit from interacting with other children. They learn many good things (and some bad things) from each other, but all of it is important to their normal, healthy development.

If this need is not being met in your neighborhood, you can go a long way towards making things better for your child with just the contact he gets with other children while at the home of a co-op sitter. In contrast to a day care environment, the sitter has children of her own for yours to play with, and because she is only watching a few children, she can give them more individual attention—resulting in a less frenetic situation. There will be different toys to play with and some different house rules and regulations to adjust to. This is usually quite stimulating and exciting for a small child. A bonus is that this early exposure and adjustment to different environments often works to everyone's further advantage later. Many parents have found that their children experience an easier transition to nursery school and kindergarten as a result of this early experience in a co-op.

Desire not to inconvenience or burden friends or family.

Most parents dislike imposing on friends or relatives whenever they need a sitter. And with good reason. Although caring friends and relatives will probably not refuse to sit if they are available, most would surely appreciate being asked only on occasion, rather than being relied upon as a primary source of babysitting.

In a co-op, the members are free to decline to sit if it is inconvenient for them. And when someone says no, there is almost always someone else to call who will say yes.

To keep the family together.

A co-op can help you to avoid turning one parent into a babysitter so that the other can go out. This occurs in families that do not have money to spend on sitters as well as in families that have the money but can't find a sitter.

Convenience.

When a co-op member needs a sitter, all she has to do is phone the bookkeeper (this procedure is described in Chapter VIII), who then assumes responsibility and makes all further arrangements. How simple!

★　　　★　　　★　　　★　　　★

At this point you may be saying to yourself that it all sounds good—except the part about doing the return babysitting. On first thought you may question the desirability of doing the babysitting required by a co-op. In reality it turns out that many co-op members actually look forward to their turn at babysitting. Your children may even be easier to be around when they have a "guest playmate." They will often spend this time entertaining each other—leaving the sitter with time to enjoy a TV program, knit or crochet, read the newspaper, or indulge in some other relaxing activity. The sitter may even find her own child demanding less attention as a result of the visitor. Sitters find that visiting children tend

They will often spend this time entertaining each other—leaving the sitter with time to enjoy a TV program, knit or crochet, read the newspaper, or indulge in some other relaxing activity.

to behave better for them than they do for their own parents—probably because they aren't sure what they can get away with. And sitters often find that they can be much more patient and understanding with someone else's children than with their own—probably because they know they don't have to keep it up for very long.

There are other more subtle advantages to this type of babysitting arrangement. It can be enlightening to sit for a child who is older than your own and to observe the new developmental stages that your child will soon be entering. If you are currently living with a contrary two year old, it may be quite refreshing to have contact with a more mellow three year old. Or you may be longing to hold a newborn baby again but have neither the financial means nor the space to have another child around permanently. If you have the opportunity to sit with an infant, you may find yourself experiencing a satisfying treat.

Before we get on to the how-tos of setting up your own babysitting co-op, let's not overlook the easy way. There may be a co-op already organized in your area. Ask around. Check with nursery schools and churches—they may be able to refer you to one. If there is a co-op and it meets your needs, join it. If one doesn't exist, or if it exists but is not suitable to your needs or there is too long a waiting list, start a new one. Remember that if *you* are setting up the group, *you* will have full initial control over the basic requirements for members. Also, you may make the rules to fit your needs and you won't have to fit yourself into an already existing (and sometimes unsatisfactory) set of rules in an ongoing co-op. If you do decide to set up your own co-op, the first thing you will need to do is recruit other interested parents.

Let your children insert the leaflets into the mailboxes if they are old enough.

CHAPTER III

WAYS TO RECRUIT MEMBERS

Gathering the core members for your co-op is often the most difficult step. The following methods are listed to help you choose the best way for you.

Organizations and clubs. Solicit members through an organization that you belong to. Try the chapter newsletter or bulletin board or bring it up at a meeting. Chances are especially good with this method that you will gather together a group of people with many similar interests.

Neighborhood fliers. Co-ops work especially well if the members live near each other. Dropping off and picking up children is much more convenient. There is also more of an opportunity for members to get to know one another. So design an attractive flyer which describes your intent and asks people to call you. Be sure to include your name and phone number. Have enough copies made to allow you to give one to every house in your neighborhood. Then take your children out for a walk, and place a flyer in *everyone's* mailbox (even the retired couple next door may know someone who would be interested). Let your children insert the leaflets into the mailboxes if they are old enough. Then sit back and wait for the calls.

Start a small co-op and actively solicit new members. The phone didn't ring quite as often as you had expected? But you did get a few congenial people together? Set up a co-op to meet the needs of that group and then together actively recruit new members until the group is large enough to function well.

Word of mouth. Remember the old joke: the quickest way to send a message is by telephone, telegraph or tell a woman? Even if it is somewhat chauvinistic, it may be useful here. Mention your plans to everyone you know, and ask them to spread the word.

Put an announcement in one of the childbirth newsletters in your area. The American Society for Psychoprophylaxis in Obstetrics (an organization that promotes the Lamaze method of prepared childbirth) and the International Childbirth Education Association are active in most large metropolitan areas and may assist you with an announcement in their local chapter newsletter. La Leche League (an organization that is supportive of nursing mothers) is another good reference point. Find your local chapters by looking in the white pages of your phone book or by contacting their national office:

> A.S.P.O.
> 1523 L Street, N.W., Suite 410
> Washington, DC 20005

> I.C.E.A.
> P.O. Box 5852
> Milwaukee, WI 53220

> La Leche League International, Inc.
> 9616 Minneapolis Avenue
> Franklin Park, IL 60131

Women's Center. Such centers are springing up everywhere. They are especially common in large cities and college towns. Contact your local center for assistance and referrals.

Adult education classes. These classes are often sponsored by the Red Cross and offered through the local high schools.

Contact the instructor of a class for new parents.

Be bold. Befriend some mothers at the playground or supermarket and make your suggestion. If they aren't interested, ask them if they know someone who might be.

P.T.A. or nursery school. Announce your plans at the next meeting. Ask to have an announcement put in their newsletter if they have one.

Welcome Wagon. Their representative may be willing to include your flyer in the package of information they present to newcomers in your area. Look for them in the white pages of your phone book.

Doctor's office. Your pediatrician or obstetrician may be able to help you by posting a notice in the waiting room or mentioning your co-op to other patients who seem to be in need of the same type of group. Ask him (or her).

Churches. Church representatives often know of people with babysitting problems and can mention your group in their bulletins and post a notice on their nursery bulletin board.

Public bulletin boards. Though at first this may seem somewhat questionable, you will probably find that only truly interested people will bother to respond. It helps if you can give an indication of age limits, family size limits, and boundaries so that you will hear only from people who meet the qualifications for your particular group. A phone conversation should provide you with adequate information to screen out unsuitable applicants.

Women's section of newspaper. Often the Women's Page will print public service announcements. Ask if your announcement could be included.

Want-ads. This is a last resort, but not to be overlooked. Advertise under "baby furnishings" or some other appropriate category which will catch the eyes of parents.

Now that you have found some people who are interested in organizing a co-op, it is time to call them together for the first meeting.

CHAPTER IV

FIRST MEETING
Getting to Know Each Other

Look at your calendar and pick a date that is convenient for you. Mornings are best for most mothers as older children are in school and younger children are usually awake and can be transported about. Plan on having a lot of children if you set up a morning meeting because finding babysitters is the problem you are trying to solve (remember?). If you have a large group and a small living space and feel it might be best to exclude children, think about setting up the meeting in the evening when fathers and teenagers are likely to be home and available to babysit. In this case be specific about the fact that you prefer children be left at home.

In some ways it's nice to have the first meeting with both children and mothers—just so you can see who you'll be cooperating with. And because this first meeting is not full of crucial decisions, some pandemonium is acceptable. Later meetings involve making important decisions and full concentration will then be essential for the benefit of everyone. A more devious reason to leave the children at home is that the mothers may find that they really enjoy this time away from their children and may, as a result, become even more motivated to organize a co-op and assure that this new freedom occurs more often.

17

Plan to serve coffee and tea as it will perk people up and keep them alert during the meeting. Have refills available throughout the meeting. Cookies are a nice accompaniment as they are the least messy type of treat that you can offer. Everyone seems to talk easier and feel more comfortable in a group of strangers when food and drink are in hand.

WHAT TO DISCUSS

At this meeting you need to exchange names, backgrounds, family sizes and locations, and most importantly why you are

Plan on having a lot of children if you set up a morning meeting because finding babysitters is the problem you are trying to solve (remember?).

interested in forming a babysitting co-op. This should break the ice. Aim to arouse interest and motivation for having a second meeting—at which time you will get down to the nitty-gritty and pick rules and guidelines for your co-op. This is too much to expect at your first gathering. Assign someone to type a *Member Information Form* like the one on page 58 and photocopy one for each member. Pick a volunteer to have the next meeting at her home (remember—no children at this one) and then set a date and time. Plan to start the meeting as early as possible as it will be a long one.

CHAPTER V

SECOND MEETING
Selecting Rules

Don't be discouraged when some people who were at the first meeting do not show up for the second one. All it means is that you have painlessly eliminated the people who aren't really interested.

At this meeting you should accomplish the following:

(1) Select a volunteer to keep a written record of the decisions made during this meeting. She may do this most easily by marking appropriately in this book next to the rules selected.

(2) Select your rules. For this you will need to refer to Chapter VIII. Read the whole chapter aloud, rule by rule. Discuss the pros and cons of each rule and *adopt only the ones which seem appropriate to the needs of your group.* Feel free to change the wording if it works out better for you. The more rules you adopt, the clearer will be everyone's expectations and the more smoothly your co-op will run. If at a later time you wish to add or drop a rule it may be done by a majority vote at a business meeting. You can expect it to take two or three years before your rules stabilize. Even then some modifications and additions will be necessary as the needs of your group change.

(3) Assign someone to type and photocopy your rules.

A copy should be passed out to each member at the next meeting.

(4) Pass out the member information forms which are to be filled out by each member, photocopied, and then exchanged at the next meeting.

(5) Decide on a bookkeeping method (see Chapter XI).

(6) Assign someone to buy the bookkeeper's supplies and to type up your agreed upon bookkeeping procedures and make a copy for each member. The bookkeeping procedures should be passed out to each member at the next meeting.

(7) Set up the third and final organizational meeting at a different member's home. Each member should bring a loose-leaf binder to keep their co-op papers in. Members will find that they are much more organized if they keep all of their co-op papers together in one place.

CHAPTER VI

THIRD MEETING

Setting Up Members' Notebooks and Preparing to Use the Cooperative

At this meeting you should accomplish the following:

(1)   Discuss Chapter IX which has samples of all the items to be kept in each member's notebook.

(2)   Copies of the rules should be given to each member. They should be read aloud to make sure that everyone understands them.

(3)   Member information forms should be exchanged and reviewed aloud.

(4)   The bookkeeping procedures should be discussed.

(5)   The chairperson should be designated as per your selected rules.

(6)   The chairperson should collect dues.

(7)   Set up the fourth meeting to discuss babyproofing and child safety. Have it at another member's home. Each member should read *The Mother's Guide to Child Safety* by Bryson R. Kalt and Ralph Bass, published by Grosset and Dunlap, before the next meeting. The first part of this sobering book discusses how to prepare for emergencies and what to do if one occurs. The second part gives suggestions on how to avoid having such horrors happen at all. The text is written in such a way that the reader can easily identify problem areas that need correcting in

her home. It should be required reading for all co-op parents and is a good book to have your paid babysitters read, too.

Now you are ready to begin using your new, invaluable babysitting co-op! After being a member of your co-op for awhile, you will begin to realize that you are fortunate indeed to have such easy access to a quality pool of babysitters that money can't buy.

CHAPTER VII

FOURTH MEETING
Child Safety and Babyproofing

At this meeting you should accomplish the following:

(1) Discuss babyproofing your homes and eliminating hazards to children.

(2) Discuss and form a list of definite procedures to follow in case of an accident while babysitting.

(3) Discuss comprehensive liability insurance. This is included in most homeowner's and renter's insurance policies. Everyone should be instructed to check with their own insurance agent to determine if their coverage is adequate. Some co-ops require that all members be covered. Discuss this possibility to see how your group feels about it.

(4) Discuss what procedures are to be followed when a child is taken from the house by the sitter. Are walks in the neighborhood permissible? Are seat belts to be used if the children are taken in a car?, etc.

CHAPTER VIII

CHOOSING RULES

Extensive rules may appear a bit tiresome to some people. To others they represent security against being taken advantage of. Whatever your feelings—in a co-op some rules are necessary for the protection of everyone. They should be devised to ensure convenience, fairness, and to help eliminate misunderstandings by spelling out clearly what is expected of each member. Often problems will be solved through discussion at business meetings and there will be no need to make a special rule. The rules are merely the framework for your group and provide a reference point for settling disputes and eliminating confusion. Pick and choose your own set of rules from the following which were culled from a representative sampling of various types of co-ops. I doubt whether any co-op will want to use them all.

But before you select rules, decide whether you want your co-op to be a small or large one. Your choice of rules will be influenced by this decision.

THE SMALL CO-OP (10-20 FAMILIES)

Small co-ops allow for intimacy and friendship. The members' children get to know one another fairly well, and people have a feeling of cooperating with friends. Parents with infants or toddlers assimilate easiest into this type of co-op.

There must be at least 10 members to make a small co-op function, with 15 being ideal and 20 being the upper limit. With less than 10 families the co-op is not viable, although some people accept the potential inconvenience to themselves in favor of keeping the number of members limited to an exclusive group. With more than 20 families it becomes a large co-op and requires a somewhat different method of organization.

THE LARGE CO-OP (20 OR MORE FAMILIES)

Large co-ops seem to be most effective when all the members live in the same apartment building or at least on the same street block. Large co-ops which are spread over a large geographical area tend to become unmanageable. Geographical cliques usually form and the group as a whole never gets to know each other well. It is probably best to break up such an unwieldy group into two or more smaller co-ops. In the case where this many people are neighbors, however, they just naturally see each other more often and it is easier to keep in contact. The disadvantage of having a lot of members that don't know each other well seems to be outweighed by the advantage of being virtually guaranteed of getting a sitter any time one is needed.

The number of families in this type of co-op is generally not limited. A new family moving into the apartment building or neighborhood would routinely be informed of the co-op's existence and would be invited to join. This kind of co-op is relatively easy to start and to keep going.

Large co-ops often send out a *monthly tabulation sheet* (see sample on page 41). With this a short *newsletter* is sometimes included in which the chairperson mentions current problems, rules being broken, news of general interest to members, dates of meetings, names of dropped members, etc. This allows for quick communication and spares the chairperson from making numerous phone calls. Larger co-ops also tend to have *membership rosters* rather than member information forms (see sample on page 59).

★　　　★　　　★　　　★　　　★

28

Name Your Co-op.

Examples are: Rolling Hills Babysitting Co-op, Leibacher Avenue Parent Sitter Cooperative, and Married Students' Housing Sitting Club.

Most co-ops use their street, town, apartment building, or organization name in the title.

List Your Founding Date.

Purpose.

Compose a statement of purpose. Pick a purpose that expresses the reasons your unique group has for setting up a babysitting co-op. The following are some examples:

- This co-op is founded to enable the member parents to leave their children and (1) feel secure that they are being well-cared for, (2) save money by exchanging babysitting time rather than money, and (3) not feel as though they are imposing on someone.

- All members of the co-op shall have equal rights and responsibilities.

- This co-op offers responsible and available childcare on an irregular and temporary basis.

- The success of any cooperative is dependent upon the responsible participation of its members. By learning and following the rules of operation, each member can assure that this co-op adequately serves the needs of all the members.

Definitions:
   A. *Gadder*—the person leaving children in a sitter's care.
   B. *Sitter*—the person caring for the gadder's children.

I.   MEMBERSHIP REQUIREMENTS
   A.   Boundaries:_____.
   [For a small co-op you will want narrow boundaries. For example, you may want to limit membership to families living in a certain housing project, living on any of a number of named streets, etc. If all your members have cars and don't mind driving greater distances, the boundaries could be extended to include a section of

a city—example, the northern part of . . .]

B.   Size: Limited to _____ active members.

[For a small co-op, 15-20 member families is a workable number. This number will usually assure you of finding a sitter when you need one. If you have less than 15 members, sometimes nobody will be available to sit. More than 20 members makes for a less closely-knit group, with a greater chance of having members who are just casually acquainted. Often when groups start enlarging or gathering a long waiting list, they will splinter into two or three smaller groups organized by area of residence or number of children. Many large co-ops have no limit on the number of members they will take.]

C.   New Members.

    1. Names are submitted to the chairperson

[The chairperson will keep a waiting list in the co-op books. See page 66.]/

    2. A new member's children may not be older than the eldest child in the co-op.

[This is where to designate age limitations. This rule as stated is practical only in a small co-op, where all members have infants or toddlers. After awhile new babies are born into co-op families, the first children get older, and the reasons for this rule become invalid. Initially, in a small co-op, it is nice to have the kids the same age. Later, when the kids are older, it won't matter as much. Another reason to consider this rule is that it is generally easier and safer if parents care for children in an age group that they are familiar with. For example: a mother of one infant may not yet have baby-proofed her home and may have no play equipment for older children. But a mother of a five-year-old would probably have little trouble caring for an infant. This is an important reason that some co-ops wish to keep the children in a similar age grouping. In larger co-ops, with no age restriction, this difficulty can be eased for first-time mothers with infants by having them always go to the gadder's house to sit.]

    3. New member families may have no more than _____ children.

[Some co-ops start out with each family having one child and evolve into families with two and more children. Starting a "young" co-op in which everyone has just one infant

or toddler is quite easy to do. Many co-ops set no limits on the number of children in a family and offer no bonuses for watching a greater number of children than your own. This system seems workable only because in larger families most of the children will be old enough to basically take care of themselves and the sitter's job is mainly supervision. Because more extensive care is necessary with babies, some co-ops offer bonuses for watching an infant.]

4. Prospective members will receive a copy of the rules to read before the interview/meeting with the chairperson.

5. New members must accept the rules as is.

6. New members must display a cooperative attitude.

[It must be made very clear to new members that they must be willing to sit whenever they are asked, unless it is truly inconvenient. People who are available to sit only when caught in the right mood waste time for everyone—especially the bookkeeper.]

7. A prospective member is interviewed by the chairperson and a co-op member who does not know her. The bookkeeper will serve in this role except in the case where she already knows the prospective member.

[This is to assure general agreement on admitting a particular person. Many co-ops eliminate this rule and will accept anyone who is recommended by another member, and some will accept anyone who applies—with no qualifications.]

8. Final decision for accepting a prospective member will rest with the majority vote of co-op members after meeting the prospective member at a "playgroup" gathering.

[This rule goes hand-in-hand with No. 7 but is not necessary unless your co-op sees an advantage to this extensive screening. The playgroup meeting, which can be conveniently held at a park playground, allows all members to be involved and gives the prospective member herself a chance to assess the mothers and children in the co-op. Some co-ops prefer to meet the prospective member without the children and hold a "coffee" for this purpose. This is best held at the chair-

*person's home at night, so that the children will be able to
stay home with daddy or a babysitter. If you choose to
adopt No. 7 and No. 8, your co-op may wish to overlook
them in the case where a member knows the prospective
member well and can assure the membership that their children will be well cared for by her.]*

9. A new member will not serve as bookkeeper or
chairperson until after being an active member for
one year.

*[The bookkeeper and chairperson have responsible and de-
manding jobs. It is essential that a member understand what
is going on before either of these jobs becomes her responsibility. Some co-ops do not have this requirement at all,
and some have a lesser time requirement of three to six
months.]*

10. One sit is required before using the co-op for
the first time.

*[This is an initiation. Some co-ops require a new member to
sit for ten hours before she can use its services. They then
bank these ten hours for the time when the person quits.
The co-op is then somewhat assured that the member won't
quit with a large debt. The ten hours are not counted in
monthly totals.]*

11. No prospective member may attend a business
meeting.

*[Business meetings are usually very busy. There is no time
to get properly acquainted with a prospective member. Also,
a lot of time would be wasted explaining things that are being discussed, and then the person may choose not to join
anyway. Keep screenings to playgroup or coffee situations.]*

12. New member will photocopy the rules, member information forms, and all other pertinent papers
on her own time and at her own expense. She will
fill out her member information form and distribute
a copy to each member. In co-ops using a membership roster, she will notify each member to add her
name to their roster.

*[This is to offset the expense of a new member dropping
out quickly. The financial investment and time spent in
photocopying may make a person think twice if they're not
sure they want to join.]*

13. A new member will begin using the co-op on the first day of the month following her acceptance. *[This is to facilitate bookkeeping. If the bookkeeper isn't inconvenienced, the new member could begin using the co-op at any time.)*

D. Medical Care and Home Safety.

1. The children of each member must be enrolled in an immunization program.
[Many co-ops do not require this; they take it for granted. Most cities offer free public health services and immunization programs, so every member—no matter what their income—should be able to meet this requirement.]

2. Each member shall carry a comprehensive homeowner's or renter's insurance policy, including minimum liability.
[Again, many co-ops do not require this. The pros and cons of making this a rule are worth discussing thoroughly.]

3. Each gadder shall leave a *medical treatment release form* with the sitter.
[This form might also be photocopied for members to keep in their respective notebooks. Check with your own doctors as you may be able to simplify this by having each member file a medical treatment release form with their doctor's office. See samples on pages 60 and 61.]

4. A member shall neither sit nor ask for a sitter when there is a contagious illness in her home. Any illness, no matter how minor, should be discussed between sitter and gadder before the sit occurs. Members may at any time refuse to sit due to a child's illness.
[Discuss the exception of allergies and non-contagious maladies. You will probably find that the subject of colds is quite a controversial one among parents of infants and toddlers. Current medical opinion leans toward saying that after three days of a runny nose the cold is no longer to be considered contagious. Discuss this topic thoroughly to determine what your co-op's definition of a cold will be. Check with your own doctors for their opinions.]

E. Finances.
Upon joining the co-op, members shall be required to

33

pay dues of $1. Further dues will be collected as needed. This sum will cover clerical expenses and other payments required for the operation of the co-op.

[Depending on the current rate of inflation and the needs of your co-op, you may need to set this rate higher. Special collections can be taken separately for special occasions. This minimizes the amount of money in the co-op treasury thus simplifying the accounting.]

F.   Business Meetings.

1.   Business meetings will be held every three months at the chairperson's home. The purpose will be to discuss co-op business, settle finances, and introduce new members. The chairperson will notify all members of the meeting at least two weeks in advance.

[This is the time to discuss problems, gripes, change rules, etc. There is usually plenty of time left over to socialize. Some co-ops schedule a special speaker or discussion topic for after the business meeting. It's best to hold these meetings at night when fathers or teenagers are more likely to be available to babysit. Some large co-ops find that one or two meetings per year are adequate. The smaller co-ops generally require more meetings (three or four per year) and reap the benefit of having a few more opportunities to get to know one another better. Generally the hostess for this meeting will have dessert and coffee available while people are gathering. Some co-ops like to also serve wine when the tension level promises to be high.]

2.   Two hours are deducted from members who do not attend. These hours are credited to *Jane Doe.*

[You must have some sort of effective penalty for not attending business meetings. It is very time-consuming for the chairperson to later give absentees a synopsis of the meeting, and she should not be expected to do this except under extenuating circumstances. You may wish to impose this penalty indiscriminately or you may wish to soften it by making stated exceptions, or you may wish to leave imposing of the penalty to the discretion of the chairperson. Jane Doe is is a fictitious member who absorbs all surplus debits and credits in the bookkeeping.]

3.   Minutes will be recorded by the previous chairperson.

4.   Any member may bring up a complaint at a

business meeting if she has already made an attempt to settle it with the chairperson and is not satisfied with the result. It must, however, first be placed on the agenda.

5. Rules may be amended or dropped and new ones may be added, with a simple majority vote of the total membership.

[You may wish to change this to a 2/3 majority of the total membership, or base the majority on the number of members present. Some co-ops find that occasionally they need to take a phone or mail ballot on an important issue that arises between scheduled meetings.]

6. Member information forms shall be updated.

[Go through the information forms one by one, allowing each member to mention any changes that are needed on her form, while the other members record these changes on their copies of her member information form.]

7. Date for a social get-together will be set and tentatively planned.

[Some co-ops have regular family get-togethers. A pot luck, picnic, or "adults only" party provide an opportunity for the members to socialize with each other. These social events can be conveniently planned to occur between scheduled business meetings.]

II. OFFICERS

A. Chairperson.

1. Serves a three month term during which she is responsible for the overall coordination of the co-op.

[This term varies from co-op to co-op. Three month terms work well with small co-ops and six month terms seem to work better with large co-ops.]

2. Is selected on a rotational basis using reverse alphabetical order of the original membership. New members are added to the bottom of the list. As each chairperson retires her name is crossed off and added to the bottom of the list. Any member may choose to skip her turn.

[Some co-ops prefer to elect their chairperson. If you decide to hold elections, consider using a secret ballot. A show of hands may be intimidating and embarrassing.]

3. Shall receive in compensation for her service ½ hour credit from each member for each month she serves. This will be credited to her by the bookkeeper at the beginning of each month.

4. Presides at business meetings and sets up the agenda.

[An agenda allows the chairperson to plan the order of topics for discussion. With thought this can often make the meeting run more smoothly. The chairperson should write down topics for discussion as they are mentioned to her. When she calls to remind each member of the business meeting, she should ask if there is anything to be added to the agenda. These items are raised anonymously at meetings.]

5. Reminds members of scheduled or cancelled meetings. Informs absent members of the minutes of the missed business meeting.

6. Shall keep the co-op monies and be responsible for collecting and recording all dues. She shall dispense funds after approval by the membership at a business meeting.

[A sample accounting system appears on page 66. Larger co-ops sometimes open checking accounts to help keep their records accurate.]

7. Notes any changes, corrections, or additions to the master set of rules kept in the co-op books—dating each as they are amended. She is responsible for retyping and photocopying the rules when excessive

CHAIRPERSON ROSTER

~~Adean~~
~~Robin~~
Joan (present chairperson)
Yoshiko
Elayne
Teri
Sabra
Carole
Merry
Eleanor
~~Eva~~ (quit)
Dee (new member)
Adean (retired chairperson)
Robin (retired chairperson)
Diane (new member)

changes warrant it.

[In co-ops which use membership rosters, the chairperson usually is responsible for preparing and distributing updated rosters. A sample roster appears on page 59.]

8. Will keep the co-op books up to date and in order.

9. Acts as a social organizer for the co-op. Will set up at least one social function during her term.

[Not many co-ops have this rule. Formalizing it into a rule, however, makes it more likely for these social events to occur. Family picnics are a favorite during the summer. "Adults only" parties are popular during the Christmas holiday season—but how will everyone find babysitters?]

10. Audits bookkeeper's books during the second month of term or whenever necessary.

[This helps avoid the sticky mess of long-unbalanced books.]

11. Oversees general enforcement of the rules. Arbitrates disputes and relaxes or adjusts rules in exceptional cases. Acts upon complaints. Consultation with the preceding chairperson is encouraged when problems arise.

[Altercations between individual members should be resolved privately if possible. Only as a last resort should they be brought up at a business meeting. Some large co-ops provide a grievance committee consisting of the chairperson, bookkeeper, and occasionally another member. People are less likely to be petty and bothersome if a committee has to meet in order to hear their complaint. This option would best be used only if there are an unreasonable amount of complaints being made.]

12. Handles screening and admittance of new members.

[A sample procedure appears on page 65.]

13. Takes minutes for the business meeting following her term as chairperson.

14. Performs any other duties relating to the operation of the co-op as are necessary and which are not specifically assigned to someone else.

B. Bookkeeper.

1. Each member serves a one-month term on a ro-

Elayne	November 19..
Merry	December
Yoshiko	January 19..
Eleanor	February
Adean	March
Dee	April
Carole	May
Robin	June
Teri	July
Joan	August
Sabra	September
Diane	October

tational basis by alphabetical order of the original membership. New members are added to the bottom of the list. As each bookkeeper finishes her turn, her name will be crossed off and added to the bottom of the list. Any member may choose to skip or trade her turn if unable to serve during her assigned month.

[Some co-ops rotate this job alphabetically according to their current membership list. New members are then inserted into the sequence based on their last name. This method proves faulty if a new member becomes bookkeeper soon after she joins and then drops out. She ends up leaving the co-op having accrued quite a few hours. In large co-ops it is less confusing if the bookkeeper's job does not rotate among the members. These co-ops often select someone who has had bookkeeping experience or who enjoys math, and she usually keeps the job for at least a three to four month period.]

2. Receives one hour credit per month from each member in compensation for her services.

[In large co-ops where the bookkeeper doesn't have to call for sitters, she often receives only ½ hour credit per month from each member.]

3. Obtains a sitter when given 36 hours notice. Finds a sitter within 24 hours of the request or calls the the gadder to explain the difficulty.

[You may also want to stipulate that the bookkeeper attempt to match up children of the same age and/or people that live close to each other—and then of these candidates, call first the person who is most in debt. In large co-ops members usually call for their own sitters.]

4. Keeps a record of sits reported to her and verifies bookkeeping totals with members at the end of the month.

In large co-ops members usually call for their own sitters.

39

[See Chapter XI for detailed bookkeeping procedures. The job of bookkeeper is time-consuming and complicated in a large co-op and also in a small co-op which is used frequently. Your co-op may wish to consider purchasing an inexpensive calculator to be kept with the bookkeeping records. This will make the job easier, more enjoyable, and—most importantly—more accurate. And you need not eliminate from the job of bookkeeper people who are "afraid" of math—just those who are "afraid" of calculators! In large co-ops the bookkeeper typically mails each member a monthly tabulation sheet *of everyone's debits and credits. Also, in some large co-ops members notify the bookkeeper of sits done by depositing* hour sheets *in her mailbox rather than by calling her. Each member should have a supply of these forms. The bookkeeper will keep a supply available at all times. The sitter is responsible for filling out one of these forms each time she sits and then returning it to the bookkeeper to be recorded.]*

HOUR SHEET

Gadder: _____

Date: _____

From: _____ To: _____

Regular hours: _____

Bonus hours: _____

Total hours: _____

Sitter: _____

5. Notifies members of who the next bookkeeper will be and the daily hours the new bookkeeper prefers to be called.

6. If necessary she explains the bookkeeping procedures to the next bookkeeper.

7. Notifies each member if she will be unavailable for more than two consecutive days during her term as bookkeeper. If a person will be unavailable during a large portion of her month as bookkeeper, she should trade with the next scheduled bookkeeper who is available and notify each member of this change.

8. Will keep track of and notify the chairperson of any member who has an excessive debit balance.

9. Calls all members at the middle of the month if any member is deeply in debt and needs to receive priority on calls for sits.

III. TIMEKEEPING.

  A. Time is calculated to the nearest ½ hour. Time less

Monthly Tabulation Sheet - May

June bookkeeper: Robin   Chairperson: Adean

	April balance	May credit	May debit	May balance
Eleanor	−½	+16	−18	−2½
Eva	−3	+17½	−14½	0
Adean	−4½	+20	−22½	−7
Dee	0	+20½	−18	+2½
Carole	+4½	+17	−16	+5½
Robin	+8	+9½	−19	−1½
Teri	−1½	+38½	−32	+5
Joan	−4	+11½	−9	−1½
Sabra	+3	+13½	−17½	−1
Elayne	−4	+4	−6	−6
Merry	+½	+16½	−10½	+6½
Yoshiko	−7½	+12	−13½	−9
Jane Doe	+9	0	0	+9
		+196½	−196½	
for questions call May bookkeeper:	Carole			

*Used primarily in large co-ops in which members arrange their own sits,
the monthly tabulation sheet serves the purpose of notifying members
of their total monthly usage of the co-op as well as their end-of-the-
month balance. Members will refer to this list to determine who most
needs to be called to do sits.*

than ½ hour is calculated by rounding off: 1-14 minutes = no credit, 15-30 minutes = ½ hour of credit.

[Your co-op may prefer to calculate time to the nearest ¼ hour if members don't mind the added arithmetic. Some co-ops use a point system: 15 minutes = 1 point, ½ hour = 2 points, 45 minutes = 3 points, 1 hour = 4 points. The point system is considered to be easier to tabulate.]

B. No member shall accumulate a debit of over 20 hours. Exceptions are overnight and full weekend sits or special permission from the chairperson for extenuating circumstances. If a member does accumulate a debit of over 20 hours, she shall refrain from using the co-op until she has reduced this debit to below 20 hours. Any member who reaches this total will be warned by the bookkeeper, and the total debit must be reduced to below 20 hours within one month of the warning. Failure to do so will result in suspension of membership and payment by the delinquent member at the rate of $1 per hour owed. The bookkeeper shall notify all members to remove this member's name from their membership rosters.

[A cutoff for debt is necessary—especially in small co-ops. The most important reason is that a member who is deeply in debt may quit, causing a substantial loss of hours to the co-op. Some co-ops restrict full-time working mothers to a ten hour debit because they find that they generally have a harder time fitting a return sit into their schedule. If the father is not working full time and is willing to sit, this rule may be waived.]

C. In the sitter's home, time is measured from the time the gadder leaves to the time she returns. In the gadder's home, time is measured from the time the sitter was asked to come (or, if she is late, from the time she arrives) to the time the gadder returns.

[Make this rule clear to everyone. There is a lot of pleasant socializing done when people drop off and pick up their children. Most co-ops feel that this time should not be charged to anyone. But some co-ops do count time from the gadder's arrival at the sitter's home to her ultimate departure. This seems to be an acceptable rule only in co-ops where the emphasis is on a business-like group and not on a social one.]

D.   Bonus Hours.

    1. If the sitter is requested to pick up and/or deliver

the gadder's children, she earns ½ hour credit for each service.

2. Members with two children are charged time and a half.

[This rules seems appropriate for co-ops with many young children because of the accompanying care they require, or in a co-op where most of the members have only one child. For co-ops with larger, older families, the rule becomes unnecessary, as the kids mostly take care of themselves. Also, co-ops that adopt the rule of going to the gadder's home for night sits find that this rule is unnecessary.]

3. Double time will be charged between 5—7 p.m. and after midnight.

[This rule is usually used only in co-ops where the sitting is done in the gadder's home. The reasoning is that dinner time and after midnight sits are either hectic or tiring and compensation should be made for this. Co-ops that do adopt this rule usually mean to discourage people from asking for a sitter during these hours. In co-ops where the sitting at night is done in the sitter's home and where people have gotten to know and trust each other, giving the gadder a key eliminates the problem of waiting up for the gadder's return. The gadder can then return and gather up her children while the sitter sleeps.]

4. If a non-member's child is to be included in a sit along with a member's child, double time is credited and debited or the member is charged at the regular co-op exchange rate and the non-member pays $1 per hour at the discretion of the sitter.

[Make the $1 per hour whatever the current going rate for sitters is in your area. No member should be expected to accept a sit with non-member children unless she wants to.]

5. If the sitter serves lunch or dinner in her own home, she receives a bonus: ½ hour for lunch, 1 hour for dinner.

[This rule may be omitted unless sitting during mealtimes becomes a problem. It should be left to the sitter to invite a visiting child to eat with her family. This should be arranged at the time when she confirms the sit with the gadder. Otherwise, the gadder should provide any necessary food.]

6. Double time may be charged if the gadder returns

home past the previously established ending time.
[This rule would apply only in the case where the sitter has been greatly inconvenienced by a breach of promise.]

7. If two members use a sitter simultaneously, each member pays regular time and the sitter receives double time. Multiple sits earn multiple credits.
[Sometimes two members want to go someplace together and want to leave their children in the same place for convenience. And sometimes only one person in the co-op is available to sit at a particular time. The person most in debt should be given first opportunity to do a multiple sit.]

IV. GENERAL RULES.

A. Each member keeps a record of her own hours so that discrepancies can be resolved with the bookkeeper.
[The bookkeeper can get in quite a bind if she has a mistake in her calculations and members have not kept track of their hours. See page 57 for a sample tally sheet.]

B. Members most in debt are called first for sits.

C. Any member may refuse to sit for any reason.
[This rule covers personality conflicts. People will sometimes want to refuse to sit for someone they don't get along with. Do discuss the idea that the sitter should have the option of rejecting a sit for whatever reason she chooses—including this one. Everyone will benefit if this option is cited in the rules, as not many people care to be forced into involvement with someone whom they dislike or who dislikes them. And sometimes people carry over a dislike for a parent to her innocent children, and this is both unfair to the children and undesirable for the/co-op.]

D. A member in debt should not refuse more than five sits in a row unless there are unusual circumstances which are approved by the chairperson. Such continuous refusal will cause reevaluation of her membership status.
[A member owing hours should go out of her way to take any sit she is asked to do. If she is asked to sit but doesn't owe hours, she might reasonably choose to be a little more selective about which sits she accepts.]

E. Members should give the chairperson any suggestions and complaints, which will be handled promptly and discussed at the business meetings when of interest to the group.

F. If disciplinary measures are indicated for a child, the gadder and sitter should discuss the situation as soon as possible. Discipline should be verbal rather than physical, unless the child's mother gives specific instructions to the contrary. Mothers should be told if their child's behavior has created problems.

[Often, parents who discipline by spanking don't want anyone else to spank their children. To avoid big problems—don't ever spank someone else's child. But do tell the mother if her child has been naughty, and do let a child know verbally if you don't care for his behavior.]

G.   A member is responsible for any breakage occuring in her home.

[Better put away that priceless vase, even if your own child has been trained to stay away from it. What kind of outing would it be if the gadder came home and found that her child had broken an expensive item and she was expected to replace it? She wasn't even there to prevent it! In this case it would have been a lot cheaper to hire a babysitter! The mother in charge is responsible to see that these things don't happen or to accept financial responsibility if they do happen. The only time the mother in charge is not financially responsible is when she is sitting at the gadder's home. This rule should help save a few friendships and ease over some potentially sticky situations.]

H.   It is suggested that members have comprehensive liability insurance for their own protection against any injuries to a visiting child. The co-op does not hold itself responsible as a group.

V.   RULES FOR GADDER.

A.   To request a sitter, phone the bookkeeper at least 36 hours in advance. With less notice, obtain your own sitter, remembering to call first those members who are most in debt. Call the bookkeeper to obtain their names.

[Unrealistic demands on the bookkeeper are eliminated by this rule. It also serves to help people get better acquainted with one another. It is always tempting to call a friend first, but members should be encouraged to avoid that. This rule must be regularly followed or one member may find herself deeply in debt and wanting to pay back her hours so that she may use the co-op more but is unable to do so because of lack of sitting opportunities. If a person is being avoided for a legitimate reason—i.e. inability to sit with children—then the situation should be reviewed by the chairperson and, if warranted, by the entire membership. Possibly the person should be asked to give up her membership in the co-op. It sounds harsh, but it is really the only sensible solution. However, even if

*left to her own devices, an incompatible member will usually quit
by her own choice in response to group pressure. In large co-ops,
members often arrange for their own sits, using the monthly tabulation sheet as a guide to who is most in debt.]*

B.   If it is necessary to cancel a sit, it may be done without penalty up to the day prior to the arranged sit. However, if the sit is cancelled on the day of the sit, the gadder is penalized two hours which will be credited to the
sitter as compensation for the inconvenience.

*[Breaches of common courtesy make this rule necessary. Not sur-
prisingly, without this rule people will sometimes be very discour-
teous. Members must realize that the sitter is planning her own
schedule around the prearranged hours of the sit. Because of her
responsibility to the gadder, she may find herself occasionally in
the position of having to deny herself a social opportunity that
comes up after she has commited herself to the sit—although she
may get out of the sit if absolutely necessary (see rule VI., D.). If
the sitter feels that the reason given is a worthy one and she has
not been greatly inconvenienced, she may choose to decline imposing the penalty. This should be left up to the sitter's discretion.]*

C.   Prepare children in advance so that they will be
aware that they are going to be left.

*[Children can be psychologically oriented towards enjoying their
"visit" out. Remind them of some things that they particularly
like at the sitter's home—a favorite toy, the new baby, a swing set,
etc. This allows them to anticipate the visit and think of it as a fun
time rather than as "Mommy is leaving me!" And all members
should be aware that most children who cry when their parents
leave, quit very soon after the door is closed. They just want to
keep their parents there as long as they will stay.]*

D.   Provide food, diapers, bottles, "lovies" (blankets,
pacifiers, teddy bears, a favorite toy, etc.).

*[Some gadders occasionally bring along special treats for their own
and the sitter's children—bunny cookies at Easter, bubbles to blow
outside on a nice day, a special bedtime treat, etc. This can make
special fun for everyone. Children over three often won't need to
bring any of their own toys along. They usually look forward to
the opportunity to play with the "new" toys at the sitter's home.]*

E.   Phone the sitter if you are going to be more than ½
hour later in arriving, or more than 1 hour later in returning, than was agreed upon.

*[In the case of a night sit in the sitter's home, you may find this
rule unnecessary.]*

Rule V., D: Provide food, diapers, bottles, "lovies" (blankets, pacifiers, teddy bears, a favorite toy, etc.).

F.   Leave a phone number where you may be reached and, if possible, emergency numbers.

G.   If a change of plans requires that a sitter be available earlier than arranged and the sitter can't accommodate it, the gadder must make her own arrangement for another sitter.

H.   Tell the sitter if someone other than the gadder is to pick up the children. The sitter must *under no circumstances* release the children to anyone other than the known mother or father unless special arrangements are made beforehand.

VI.   RULES FOR THE SITTER

A.   Promptly confirm date and time of sit with the gadder.

B.   Tell the gadder in advance if there will be any unusual circumstances (husband sitting alone, presence of guests in the house, multiple sit, etc.). The gadder may decline to use the sitter if she does not approve.
[Parents with newborns or children prone to illness may wish to keep their child's contacts to a minimum. And in the case of a multiple sit, sometimes a particular child doesn't get along with another child. Keeping them apart may be in everyone's best interest.]

C.   It is expected that the sitter will be the mother, unless otherwise prearranged with the people involved.

D.   If the sitter must cancel, she may do so without penalty up to the day prior to the arranged sit. However, if she cancels on the day of the sit, she incurs a penalty of 4 hours to be credited to the gadder under the following circumstances:

1. If the gadder is unable to find a substitute sitter within the co-op and must stay home.

2. If the co-op sitter is only able to find a paid sitter as a substitute, the penalty will act as a consolation for the unexpected expense.

However, if the substitute is found from the membership, there will be no penalty.
[Or you may wish to stipulate that the expense be split by the sitter and gadder if a paid sitter becomes necessary. Gadders who

have not been too inconvenienced may choose to forego this penalty if it is felt that the sitter had a justifiable reason for cancelling the sit (children do get seriously ill, and sometimes personal disasters strike at inconvenient times). In the case where a sitter who cancels has to pay for the gadder's paid sitter, the co-op sitter is credited and the gadder is debited the hours of the sit. In effect this means the co-op sitter will lose some money but she will be credited with the time she pays for just as if she actually did the sit.]

E. The sitter will not take the gadder's children from her home without prior discussion with, and approval of, the gadder, except in an extreme emergency.
[This helps to avoid unfortunate accidents outside the home. Also, sometimes a gadder returns earlier than expected. If her child is not where he is supposed to be, worry and inconvenience may result.]

F. At the end of the sit verify total hours with the gadder. Within three days report this total to the bookkeeper. On the last day of the month, however, report the sit on the following day. Once the books are closed, credit will be lost for hours not reported on time.
[This is to make it possible for the bookkeeper to keep an accurate record of each member's current debit and credit totals.]

G. It is the sitter's responsibility to provide proper sleeping arrangements for the gadder's children if the sit occurs in the sitter's home.
[Portable cribs or playpens are essential for children under three; bunk beds or sleeping bags are fine for older children. Older children enjoy bringing their own sleeping bag along and have no trouble sleeping in it on a carpeted or padded floor. The sitter's and gadder's children can be put in the same room for an enjoyable slumber party. The cutesie bags that unzip to make a comforter for the child's bed at home are an especially wise selection for co-op parents.]

H. Note all messages and *never* open the door to anyone you don't know while the family is away.
[Nowadays this is common sense. Take for example this common method of burglary: The gadding parents may unwittingly give their key ring to a parking lot attendant. It is possible for the attendant or an accomplice to copy the keys, go to the car's registered address (usually available from the registration slip kept in the glove compartment), and attempt to burglarize the owner's residence. Be cautious.]

Older children enjoy bringing their own sleeping bag along and have no trouble sleeping in it on a carpeted or padded floor.

I. All special instructions will be left to the arrangement of the gadder, such as the giving of medicine.

J. During daytime hours, the sitter shall personally supervise any outdoor play involving the children she is responsible for. This means that she must accompany the children *wherever they go outdoors.* This is the rule regardless of the age of the child, unless by prior arrangement to the contrary with the gadder.

K. *Never* leave the children alone.

VII. TYPES OF SITS.

A.   Daytime sits.
Usually done in the sitter's home. May be done in either home at the discretion of the families involved.

B.   Nighttime sits.

1. Usually done in the gadder's home. May be done in either home at the discretion of the families involved.
[In some co-ops—especially ones where members have only one small child—it works well to have the gadder drop off her child at the sitter's home. With older children and larger numbers of children, it seems to work best to have them bedded down in their own home. An alternative is to have the children dropped off at the sitter's home with the agreement that at bedtime the sitter will return them to the gadder's home and bed them down there, remaining in the gadder's home until the end of the sit. Some people prefer to go to the gadder's home to sit and find it a good time to catch up on reading, mending, letter writing, or just to relax and watch TV, undistracted by dishes that need washing or other nagging chores left undone in their own homes.]

2. Children should be fed and ready for bed if possible.
[Depending on your group, you may or may not need this rule. With some children, eating and dressing for bed is a calming ritual. When the sit occurs in the sitter's home she may enjoy inviting the gadder's child to eat with her family —a treat the children usually enjoy immensely.]

3. If done at the gadder's home, the gadder should
   a. Ask if the sitter prefers pets out of the house

or room.

b. Leave porch light on, provide coffee, snacks, flashlight, blanket, pillow, and show the sitter how to turn on the heat.

c. Make sure the sitter gets safely to her car when she leaves.

d. Give the sitter ½ hour extra credit for travel time.

[This is done only in co-ops where night sits are usually done in the sitter's home.]

[It is nice if the gadder has some special toys available for her children to use only when they have a babysitter. This gives the kids something to look forward to and usually makes their parents' parting quite painless.]

C. Overnight sits.

Done in the sitter's home. For the time period between 7 p.m. and 9 a.m. the sitter will be given a flat fee of eight hours credit whether or not the gadder's child is there the whole time or not. Hours of the sit that occur before 7 p.m. or after 9 a.m. will be charged at the regular co-op rate.

[If you live very close to each other, you may consider changing this rule to exclude the hours between midnight and when the child rises in the morning from the recorded/time. Older children could then get dressed and be walked home, or the sitter could call the parents to pick them up.]

D. Full weekend sits.

Gadder must have a minimum of 12 hours credit before using a weekend sit.

Friday night: Time is counted from when the child arrives until he goes to sleep.

Saturday: 12 hours allotted.

Sunday: Time is counted from when the child awakes until the parents return.

[Members who know each other well may prefer to just trade a weekend for a weekend and not get technical about the exact number of hours. This is usually arranged independently of the co-op's bookkeeping system. Also, it is sometimes hard for a member to amass a surplus of 12 hours credit. For this reason a member should call the bookkeeper a few weeks ahead of her scheduled

weekend away, and ask the bookkeeper to guide extra sits her way so that she can accumulate the necessary plus hours.]

VIII. INACTIVITY.

A. Notify bookkeeper when on vacation or unavailable for any length of time.
[This is necessary primarily in the case where someone is in debt and will be called frequently for sits. This notification spares the bookkeeper some wasted effort.]

B. After three months of inactivity (neither sitting nor gadding) the member will be asked to balance out her hours and then will be dropped.

C. Reinstatement may be made only after the membership evaluates the reasons for inactivity.

D. A member wishing to relinquish her membership should try to get her debits and credits to balance out by notifying the bookkeeper as far in advance as possible. If unable to do so, she pays the co-op $1 per hour owed.
[Make the per hour charge whatever the current sitting rate is in your area.]

E. A Jane Doe account is set up to receive the plus and minus hours of members leaving the co-op or being penalized. The account is set up for the purpose of balancing the books.

F. Deduction of hours for chairperson and bookkeeper will be made whether a person has used the co-op or not.
[Some co-ops allow for a deduction-free leave of absence. This tends to be unfair to the people who are chairperson and bookkeeper during the peak vacation months in the summer. Everyone should get a fair chance to earn back all the hours that they have paid to other chairpersons and bookkeepers.]

DON'T LET FRUSTRATIONS ABOUT THE RUNNING OF THE CO-OP BUILD UP WITHIN YOU. TELL THE CHAIRPERSON OR BOOKKEEPER OF YOUR COMPLAINT. THEIR JOB IS TO ACT PROMPTLY AND WILLINGLY TO RESOLVE THE PROBLEM.

CHAPTER IX

MEMBER'S NOTEBOOK

Each member needs to keep her co-op papers together in one spot—a notebook or file would be appropriate.

The following items should be kept in each member's notebook. Items preceded by an asterisk are illustrated in this chapter.

*1. Emergency data sheet.

*2. Tally sheet for itemizing all use of the co-op—both sitting and gadding—by the member.

*3. Member information forms or membership roster.

*4. Medical treatment release form.

5. Copy of the rules.

EMERGENCY DATA SHEET

ADDRESS OF RESIDENCE

POLICE

FIRE

POISON CONTROL

DOCTOR

HOSPITAL

NEIGHBOR

MEDICAL INSURANCE COMPANY AND ACCOUNT #

AMBULANCE

*WHERE GADDER MAY BE REACHED

NON-EMERGENCY DATA

CHILDREN'S BEDTIMES

SPECIAL RULES

GENERAL INFORMATION   (for example: "Jason needs a pacifier and blanket at bedtime." "Jennifer needs the light left on at bedtime.")

The gadder should leave this form near the phone when a sit occurs in her home.

---

*This may be filled in in pencil and updated before each sit.

TALLY SHEET

DATE	MEMBER'S NAME/TIME	DEBIT	CREDIT	CURRENT BALANCE
			(balance forward)	$+4\frac{1}{2}$ [1]
MAY	dues - chairperson/bookkeeper	$-\frac{1}{2}$	$+11$ [2]	$+15$
6	Merry (6^{35} - 7^{35})	-1		$+14$
8	Teri (6^{55} - 8^{50})	-2		$+12$
9	Eleznor (6^{30} - 10^{30})		$+6$ [3]	$+18$
10	Eleznor (6^{20} - 11^{30})	-5		$+13$
12	Eleanor (6^{30} - 9^{30})	-3		$+10$
20	Yoshiko (6^{45} - 9^{15})	$-2\frac{1}{2}$		$+7\frac{1}{2}$
22	Yoshiko (7^{10} - 9^{15})	-2		$+5\frac{1}{2}$ [1]
JUNE	dues	$-1\frac{1}{2}$		$+4$
2	Joan (6^{30} - 9^{30})	-3		$+1$
3	Yoshiko (6^{45} - 9)	-2		-1
10	Robin (11^{30} - 12^{35})	-1		-2

(1) End of month balance.
(2) This member was bookkeeper for May.
(3) Eleanor is charged time and a half for two children.

Twelve copies of this form will usually be enough to last a member more than a year. Totals should be checked against the bookkeeper's records at the end of the month. If the totals do not agree, track down the mistake by checking each sit you have recorded against the sits the bookkeeper has recorded for you.

MEMBER INFORMATION FORM

Name_____and_____
     (last)   (husband)   (wife)

Address_____city_____

Cross streets_____

Home phone_____Husband's work phone_____

Wife's work phone_____

Number of children_____ ____

Name   Birthdate   School

_____   _____   _____

_____   _____   _____

_____   _____   _____

Doctor's name_____Phone_____

Office address_____

Emergency instructions_____

_____

_____

_____

Allergies and instructions_____

_____

_____

Handicaps and instructions_____

_____

_____

Pets_____

Preferable sitting times_____

Best times to call_____

Additional comments_____

_____

MEMBERSHIP ROSTER

COLUMBIA SITTING CLUB

October 19..

```
*   Carolyn A.
*** (C. Clifford) 000-0000
    00 Grant Ave.
    Erik-Jan '67
    Kaiser #000-000
    Claire-Nov '70
    Kaiser #000-000
    Dr. Arnold 000-0000
    hus. 000-0000 x000 or x000

*   Judi B.
**  (Leo) 000-0000
*** 00 - 24th Street
    Lynette-April '68
    Kaiser #000-000
    Lianne-Nov '70
    Kaiser 000-000
    Dr. Stein 000-0000
    hus. 000-0000

**  Ellen B.
    (Larry) 000-0000
    000 Pine Lane
    Diana-Aug '66
    Kaiser #000-000
    Wendy-Feb '68
    Kaiser #000-0000
    hus. 000-0000
```

```
  *   - evening
  **  - Weekend days
  *** - overnights
```

This is the form that is
followed for the roster:

mother's name

husband's name, home phone

address

children's names and birthdate

children's medical number

children's doctor and his phone

husband's work phone

This form is generally used only in larger co-ops.

MEDICAL TREATMENT RELEASE FORM

AUTHORIZATION TO CONSENT TO TREATMENT OF MINOR

We, the undersigned parents/guardians of the minor/minors listed below do hereby authorize_____ and/or_____an adult person into whose care the minor has been entrusted, as an agent for the undersigned to consent to any X-ray examinations, anesthetic, medical or surgical diagnosis or treatment and hospital care which is deemed advisable by, and is to be rendered under the general or special supervision of any physician and surgeon licensed under the provision of the Medical Practice Act.

It is understood that this authorization is given in advance of any specific diagnosis, treatment or hospital care being required, but is given to provide authority and power on the part of our aforesaid agent(s) to give specific consent to any and all such diagnosis, treatment or hospital care which the aforementioned physician in the exercise of his best judgement may deem advisable.

We hereby assume all financial responsibility for such service.
Minor's name:

Birth date:

Address:

Phone:

Doctor's name:	Medical insurance and number:
Allergies:	Blood type:
Date:	Sincerely,

_____(mother)

_____(father)

60

There are several ways you may decide to use this form.

    1. *Each member will keep a signed, filled-out copy in their notebook for every child in the co-op, or*

    2. *A signed copy can be kept on file in each doctor's office with the first two spaces left blank so that they may be filled out by the sitter in an emergency.*

If you do decide to use this form, its legality must be checked with your own doctor and it may possibly need to be altered in order to be valid in your particular state.

MEDICAL TREATMENT RELEASE FORM

AUTHORITY TO OPERATE

I hereby grant authority to Dr._____to care

for my child,_____, born_____.

He has permission to administer anesthesia or perform any

operation he diagnoses as necessary or advisable in the

emergency treatment of this patient.

_____(mother) _____(date)

_____(father) _____(date)

_____(witness) _____(date)

This is a simpler form to use, but still must be checked with your own doctors for legality and suitability. The advantage to this form is that it need only be kept on file with the child's doctor. In an emergency, it should be easy to obtain from the child's file.

CHAPTER X

CHAIRPERSON'S NOTEBOOK

A special notebook should be set up in which all papers related to the co-op shall be kept. Each chairperson shall be responsible for updating the notebook during her term. The following items should be kept in the chairperson's notebook. Items preceded by an asterisk are illustrated in this chapter.

*1. Call check list (to assure notification of all members regarding co-op business).

*2. Procedure sheet for screening new members.

3. Agenda for upcoming business meeting.

4. Minutes of past meetings.

*5. Dues and expense sheet. Dues may be kept in a manila envelope in this notebook.

*6. Waiting list.

7. Extra member information forms and rule sheets for new members.

CALL CHECK LIST

	meet. 22nd	meet. 22nd change place	playgroup 15th Yoshiko	Yoshiko new member	Dec. 3 meet	Xmas party Dec. 16	meet. Jan 29		
Eleanor (phone#)	✓	✓	✓	✓	✓	✓	✓		
~~Eva~~	✓	✓							
~~Vicki~~	no answer	can't come	phone disconnect						
Adean	✓	✓	✓	✓	✓	✓	✓		
Carole	✓	✓	✓	✓	✓	✓	✓		
Robin	✓	✓	✓	✓	✓	✓	✓		
Teri	✓	✓	can't come	✓	✓	✓	✓		
Joan	✓	✓	✓	✓	✓	✓	✓		
Sabra	✓	✓	✓	✓	✓	✓	✓		
Elayne	✓	✓	can't come	✓	✓	✓	✓		
Betsy	✓	can't come	can't come	✓	can't come	✓	✓		
Merry	✓	✓	✓	✓	✓	✓	✓		
Yoshiko					✓	✓	✓		

PROCEDURE FOR SCREENING PROSPECTIVE MEMBERS

1. Follow up on waiting list as soon as there is an opening.

2. Call the prospective member and arrange a time to visit in the home--preferably at a time when her children are home.

3. Call an active member who is unacquainted with the prospective member and ask her to accompany you.

4. At the visit give the prospective member a copy of the rules. Discuss them. Discuss "babyproofing".

5. Arrange to have prospective member come to next Wednesday playgroup.

6. Call all co-op members and ask them to attend that playgroup.

7. After the playgroup meeting, contact all members who attended to determine whether prospective member is welcome to join. Do this within 24 hours.

8. Call the prospective member immediately and let her know the results.

9. If she is accepted:

   a. Give her a member information form to fill out and instruct her to have copies made and send one to each co-op member.

   b. Make her a photocopy of each of the current co-op member information forms.

   c. She will organize a notebook in which to keep her co-op papers.

   d. She will contact the next month's bookkeeper and ask to be added to the books. She will not start using the co-op until the beginning of that month.

Because screening new members is done by different people as they become chairperson, it is important to draw up some guidelines for the chairperson to follow—especially if the procedure is complicated.

DUES AND EXPENSE SHEET

DATE	ITEM	MEMBER	AMOUNT	BALANCE	
5/13	dues		+$5.75	$5.75	
5/28/74	note book & dividers for chairperson	Carole	– 1.30	+ 4.45	
7/31/74	dues from new members		+ 2.00	+ 6.45	
10/22/74	bookkeeping book	Teri	– .60	+ 5.85	
2/25/75	photocopy rules	Carole	– 2.35	+ 3.50	
3/20/75	stamps to send rules	Adean	– .50	+ 3.00	
3/20/75	dues	Adean	+ .50	+ 3.50	

WAITING LIST

DATE CONTACTED CO-OP	NAME/ADDRESS/PHONE NUMBER/ BIRTHDATE OF CHILD	WHO REFERRED/SPONSOR
6/17/74	Judy · · · girl 8/72	Carole Called 10/74 not interested
6/28/74	Yoshiko · · · boy 8/73	Carole joined 12/74
5/15	Diane · · · boy 12/72	knows most of us joined 8/75
6/75	Judy · · · 12/74	Dee

66

CHAPTER XI

BOOKKEEPING METHODS

There are several different methods of bookkeeping that are used by babysitting co-ops. Some are very simple and casual, while others are more complicated and formal. On the following pages the most common bookkeeping methods are illustrated and described. You are encouraged to read them thoughtfully and pick the one that seems to be most viable for your group.

Whatever method of bookkeeping your co-op chooses, all members should keep a personal tally sheet and record information concerning their own use of the co-op. If you choose either of the first two methods—*cards or traditional bookkeeping*—consider purchasing a pocket calculator for use by the bookkeeper.

CARDS

A large 6" x 8" lined recipe card is kept for each member. The bookkeeper records all information on the proper card and tallies as she goes. Cards are arranged in order of decreasing number of hours owed. Thus the name of the person most in debt is on the first card, and the name of the person with the most credit is on the last card. When it is time for the bookkeeper to call the members to locate a sitter, she

67

goes through the cards from front to back until she finds someone who can do the sit. The order of the cards is rearranged when someone calls in to report a completed sit. After entering the new totals, she refiles the cards into their new position. At the end of the month the bookkeeper totals the current debits and credits for each member. They should balance. When a card becomes full, it is kept in the back of the file until another card for that person is completed. It may then be discarded.

This method is the easiest I've come across. A minor drawback is that the total hours the co-op was used in any given month cannot be easily determined, unless a separate record is kept. This could be done by keeping a special index card with this information entered monthly by each bookkeeper. All co-ops will find this an expedient method of bookkeeping, but some may prefer the more traditional method.

Adean				(phone #)	
date	hours	member	debit	credit	balance
			(balance forward)		(+ 4½)
5-1	—	dues-chairperson/bookkeeper (Adean)	-½	+11	+15
5-6	6³⁵-7³⁵	Merry	-1		+14
5-8	6⁵⁵-8⁵⁰	Teri	-2		+12
5-9	6³⁰-10³⁰	Eleanor		+6	+18
5-10	6²⁰-11³⁰	Eleanor	-5		+13
5-12	6³⁰-9³⁰	Eleanor	-3		+10
5-20	6⁴⁵-9¹⁵	Yoshiko	-2½		+7½
5-22	7¹⁰-9¹⁵	Yoshiko	-2		(+5½)
6-1	—	dues-chairperson/bookkeeper	-1½		+4
6-2	6³⁰-9³⁰	Joan	-3		+1
6-3	6⁴⁵-9	Yoshiko	-2		-1
6-10	11³⁰-12⁴⁵	Robin	-1		-2

TRADITIONAL BOOKKEEPING

This method uses an accounting-type book to record information. It allows for extremely accurate, month-by-month records. A drawback is that it is more difficult for the bookkeeper to keep running totals in this type of system than it is with the cards. It requires the purchase of a *teacher's class record and roll book,* available for under $1 at most stationery stores. Illustrations in this book are done on the National brand class record and roll book, No. 33-988. Detailed procedures and samples follow.

GUIDELINES FOR TRADITIONAL BOOKKEEPING

A copy of these directions should be kept with the bookkeeper's books, to be referred to as needed.

First of the month.

1. Copy names and phone numbers along the left side of the page. Fill in dates at the top. Carry over the last month's totals to column L/T. If it is a credit, use black pencil and enter it in the upper half of the space; if it is a debit, use red pencil and enter it in the lower half of the space. Draw dark lines between names. Add in new members alphabetically.

2. Credit the bookkeeper 1 hour for every member but herself (ex.: 12 members = 11 hours credit). Debit everyone else 1 hour.

3. Credit chairperson ½ hour for every member but herself (ex.: 12 members = 5½ hours credit). Debit everyone else ½ hour.
    In sum, everyone is debited 1½ hours on the first of the month except the bookkeeper who is debited ½ hour and the chairperson who is debited 1 hour.

4. Use red pencil for debits, black pencil for credits throughout the month.

5. Maintain subtotals, changing them as people call in hours, so that you will have an accurate accounting of debits and credits. Do this in pencil.

6. Checks may be entered in the books to denote sits that have been arranged but not yet completed.

Throughout the month.

Use the *bookkeeper's worksheet,* illustrated on page 71, to record requests for sits.

End of the month.

1. Add each member's debits and put them in their debit column. *Do not add in amount in L/T column.*

2. Add each member's credits and put them in their credit column. *Do not add in amount in L/T column.*

3. Balance each member's credits and debits by calculating the sum of *L/T column, (+) credit column,* and *(−) debit column.* Put total in red or black ink in *current total column.*

4. Total credits and put at the bottom of the credit column. Total debits and put at the bottom of the debit column. If the totals balance (are equal), fine. If not, recheck for mistakes until they do balance (i.e. for every sitter who got credited an hour, there must be a gadder who got debited an hour).

5. Sum the current total column. The debits and credits should cancel, giving a sum of zero. If not, check for mistakes until these total zero.

6. The Jane Doe account is used when the balance is offset for some reason (someone leaves the co-op with a debit or credit balance, or penalties for missing a meeting). It is carried over each month.

7. Call each member and verify her balance and inform her of who the new bookkeeper will be. Give the bookkeeping books to the new bookkeeper on the first day of the month.

The following pages illustrate how the books will look during the middle and at the end of the month. A detailed explanation is given of member Teri's activity for the month.

DATE OF CALL TO BOOKKEEPER	GADDER	DATE OF SIT	DAY OF SIT	TIME OF SIT	SITTERS CALLED (CIRCLE SITTER WHO ACCEPTS)	HOURS CALLED IN (CIRCLE WHEN POSTED)
May 14	Teri	22	Th	7¹⁵-9 pm	Yoshiko	③
27	Teri	30	F	6⁴⁵-12	Eleanor	⑥
27	Adean	30	F	6⁴⁵-12	Dee	⑥
	Carole	29	Tn	9³⁰-4	Eleanor – cancelled –	
28	Eva	30	F	6³⁰-11	Robin, Merry – cancelled –	
June	Carole	2	M	6³⁰-10	Eleanor, Yoshiko, Joan	
31	Teri	2	M	"		

This form is used by the bookkeeper as she receives calls requesting and reporting sits. She may then make entries in the bookkeeping books at her convenience.

bookkeeper: Carole
Chairperson Robin

MAY 19..

		1	2	3	4	5	6	7	8	9	10	11
1	Eleanor	+										✓	
2	(phone #)	−	-1½	-6							-6		
3	Eva	+		+4			+6						
4	(phone #)	−	-1½	-3½							-2½	✓	
5	Adean	+		+5½						+10			
6	(phone #)	−	-1½		-3			-3					
7	Dee	+		+3½					+9½				
8	(phone #)	−	-1½										✓
9	Carole	+	+11								+6		
10	(phone #)	−	-½					-1		-2		✓	
11	Robin	+	+5½				+½						✓
12	(phone #)	−	-1		-6				-5				
13	Teri	+							+3	+2		✓	
14	(phone #)	−	-1½	-7						-2	-5½		
15	Joan	+			+3								
16	(phone #)	−	-1½										
17	Sabra	+		+6						+5	+2½		
18	(phone #)	−	-1½	-2½									
19	Elayne	+											
20	(phone #)	−	-1½										
21	Merry	+			+6			+1					
22	(phone #)	−	-1½				-6½						
23	Yoshiko	+											
	(phone #)	−	-1½							-7½	-4½		
	Jane Doe	+											
		−											

Explanation for Teri's entries for the first half of the month:

on the 1st — Teri is debited 1½ hours for dues.
   (Robin is credited ½ hour for being chairperson. Carole is credited 1 hour for being bookkeeper.)
on the 2nd — Teri is debited 7 hours.
   (Eva sat for Teri for 4 hours. Adean sat for Teri for 5½ hours. Teri sat for Sabra for 2½ hours. Due to space limitations, all of these transactions were entered as a net 7 hour debit for that day.)
on the 6th — Teri is credited 3 hours.
   (Teri sat for Adean for 3 hours.)

72

16	17	18	19	20	21	22	23	24	25	26	27	28	29	30	31	L/T	credit	debit	current total
																	0		
																-½		-13½	-14
																	+10		
																-3		-7½	-½
																	+15½		+3½
																-4½		-7½	
																0	+3½		+2
																		-1½	
																+4½	+17		+18
																		-3½	
																+8	+6		+2
																		-12	
																	+5		
																-1½		-14½	-11
																	+3		
																-4		-1½	-2½
																+3	+13½		+12½
																		-4	
																	0		
																-4		-1½	-5½
																+½	+7		
																		-8	-½
																	0		
																-½		-6	-13½
																+9			

on the 7th – Teri is debited 2 hours.
  (Dee sat for Teri for 2 hours.)
on the 8th – Teri is credited 2 hours.
  (Teri sat for Carole for 2 hours.)
  Teri is debited 5½ hours.
  (Adean sat for Teri for 5½ hours.)
  (This entry could also have been writ-

*ten as a debit of 3½ hours for Teri.
However, a mistake is easier to catch
if it is written out step by step.)*

on the 10th – A check appears here because
  Teri requested the bookkeeper to get
  her a sitter for this day, but the sit
  has not yet been reported.

MAY 19..

Name	±	1	2	3	4	5	6	7	8	9	10	11	12
Eleanor (phone #)	+										+5		+.
	−	-1½	-6							-6			
Eva (phone #)	+		+4			+6							
	−	-1½	-3½							-2½	-5		
Adean (phone #)	+		+5½						+10				
	−	-1½		-3			-3				-6		
Dee (phone #)	+		+3½					+9½					
	−	-1½										-3½	
Carole (phone #)	+	+11								+6			
	−	-½					-1		-2		-5		-
Robin (phone #)	+	+5½				+½						+3½	
	−	-1		-6				-5					
Teri (phone #)	+						+3		+2		+11		
	−	-1½	-7					-2	-5½				
Joan (phone #)	+		+3										
	−	-1½											
Sabra (phone #)	+		+6					+5		+2½			
	−	-1½	-2½										
Elayne (phone #)	+												
	−	-1½											
Merry (phone #)	+		+6			+1							
	−	-1½				-6½							
Yoshiko (phone #)	+												
	−	-1½						-7½	-4½				
Jane Doe	+												
	−												

Explanation for Teri's entries for the rest of the month:

on the 10th — Teri is credited 11 hours.
(Teri sat for Adean for 6 hours and for Eva for 5 hours.)

on the 14th — Teri is debited 1½ hours.
(Dee sat for Teri for 1½ hours.)

on the 15th — Teri is credited 1 hour.
(Teri sat for Robin for 1 hour.)

on the 17th — Teri is debited 4½ hours.
(Eva sat for Teri for 4½ hours.)

on the 21st — Teri is credited 2 hours.
(Teri sat for Joan for 2 hours.)

on the 22nd — Teri is credited 5½ hours.
(Teri sat for Joan for 5½ hours.)
Teri is debited 1 hour.
(Yoshiko sat for Teri for 1 hour.)

on the 27th — Teri is credited 7 hours.
(Teri sat for Elayne for 4½ hours and for Yoshiko for 2½ hours.)

on the 29th — Teri is credited 7 hours.
(Teri sat for Sabra for 5 hours and for Eva for 2 hours.)

5	16	17	18	19	20	21	22	23	24	25	26	27	28	29	30	31	L/T	+ credit	− debit	current total
															+6			+16		
						-4½											-½		-18	-2½
	+4½																	+17½		0
														-2			-3		-14½	
						+4		+½										+20		
															-6		-4½		-22½	-7
															+6		0	+20½		+2½
	-5	-6																	-18	
																	+4½	+17		+5½
					-2½		-2												-16	
																	+8	+9½		
1						-4													-19	-1½
1						+2	+5½					+7		+7				+38½		+5
	-4½						-1	-½							-6	-2½	-1½		-32	
		+6														+2½		+11½		
						-2	-5½										-4		-9	-1½
																	+3	+13½		
	-1½													-5	-4				-17½	-1
															+4			+4		
												-4½					-4		-6	-6
						+4½											+½	+16½		+6½
												-2½							-10½	
	+6½				+2½		+3											+12		
																	-7½		-13½	-9
																	+9			+9
																		+196½	-196½	
													Current total					+28½	-28½	

on the 30th – Teri is debited 6 hours.
(Dee sat for Teri for 6 hours.)

on the 31st – Teri is debited 2½ hours.
(Joan sat for Teri for 2½ hours.)

At the end of the month the bookkeeper totals Teri's hours as follows:

L/T column = – 1½
credits for month = +38½
debits for month = –32
current total = + 5

PLAYMONEY OR SCRIP

$20 in play money (or whatever sum you agree upon) is given to each family when they join the co-op. The *play money/scrip* is exchanged when a sit is done. All that is needed for this form of bookkeeping is some play money or some especially made-up co-op scrip.

Each family enters the co-op with a credit. They must start to pay back their scrip before they run out of it. A disadvantage with this method is that sometimes a member needs to use the co-op a lot all at once and has no time to pay back these owed hours until later. It can get very confusing if members extend credit among each other, and then have trouble remembering who owes what. Some co-ops that use this method allow members to buy scrip from other members with "real" money at the going babysitting rate. Because this defeats one of the basic purposes of a babysitting co-op—*free* babysitting—you may wish to discourage this practice if you adopt scrip. And there can be the further confusion of members forgetting to bring along their play money or scrip to pay their sitter. The big advantage to this method of bookkeeping seems to be that no bookkeeper is necessary.

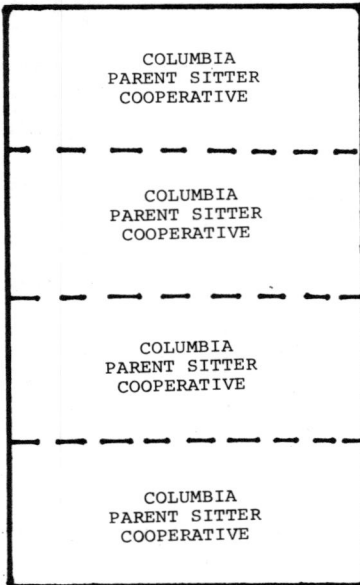

```
┌─────────────────────────────┐
│        COLUMBIA             │
│   PARENT SITTER             │
│   COOPERATIVE               │
│ ─ ─ ─ ─ ─ ─ ─ ─ ─ ─ ─ ─ ─   │
│        COLUMBIA             │
│   PARENT SITTER             │
│   COOPERATIVE               │
│ ─ ─ ─ ─ ─ ─ ─ ─ ─ ─ ─ ─ ─   │
│        COLUMBIA             │
│   PARENT SITTER             │
│   COOPERATIVE               │
│ ─ ─ ─ ─ ─ ─ ─ ─ ─ ─ ─ ─ ─   │
│        COLUMBIA             │
│   PARENT SITTER             │
│   COOPERATIVE               │
└─────────────────────────────┘
```

Sample of Scrip

Scrip often has the name of the co-op printed four times on a standard 3" x 5" recipe card. For quarter or half hours, the card may be cut.

CHAPTER XII

USING THE CO-OP FOR FUN

Once you get past the serious business of rule-making, there will be time to think about using your babysitting co-op in other ways.

Pot luck dinners and picnics will tend to be the most common type of co-op get-together. These are easy to organize and popular with most people. A member's large yard or a park are suitable meeting spots. A *hayride and weiner roast* would also be a popular outing with the children.

Your co-op may enjoy a *parents only* party occasionally. The only problem here, of course, is getting babysitters! Relatives, friends, agencies, and teenagers may be available to sit on these special occasions. Be sure to give them plenty of notice. Relatives and friends may even consider this opportunity to babysit for you to be a treat—since they are so rarely asked! A pot-luck dinner in a member's home is ideal for this type of get-together and becomes festive and fun when an ethnic food theme is used. A keg of beer or a jug of wine will add to the fun. You might consider having your party catered by a local restaurant. When a lot of people share the expense, this becomes a reasonably priced venture. Or, you may enjoy a banquet at a favorite local restaurant.

At *Christmas* a party for the kids is fun. It may be held at a park (in temperate zones), in a recreation room, at a member's home, or maybe in a church nursery, or at your local YWCA. You'll think of other spots. The kids will enjoy singing seasonal songs and exchanging presents. One co-op I know of has a daddy dress up as Santa (Santa costumes are available in Sear's Christmas "Wish Book" catalogue) and deliver presents to all the children's homes. Mommy could be Mrs. Claus and the kids could be turned into elves. What excitement for the little co-opers! Each member might like to donate ½ hour babysitting time to that special family that takes the time to play Santa during the busy holidays. You might also consider a carolling party.

How about having an *Easter* bunny deliver baskets at Easter time? Maybe some of the parents and older children can get together to dye eggs and arrange baskets before the big event.

A *toy exchange* is a good way to recycle discarded toys that are still functional. Each member can bring a toy to the business meeting. Members can trade toys when the meeting is over. The chairperson could be responsible for keeping a special toy exchange box in her home.

A co-op *playgroup* may prove workable for some members. A group of three or four is a nice size. Children will need to be of similar ages. Mothers may alternate having all of the children in their home. They have one day of being in charge and two or three days free (depending on how many kids are participating). Hours should be decided by the people participating, but 9:30 a.m.—1:30 p.m. seems to be a good time range for three year olds, with less time allowed for under-threes, and if a person must bring their child early or pick them up late, there are no irritations because the extra time can be charged to their co-op account! These playgroups are special fun because the children enjoy the different toys, snacks, and lunches at each home. Check with your library for books explaining the details of how to set up a playgroup.

A *barter system* may be worked out where talented members may exchange their non-babysitting services for babysitting credit. How would you like to trade a night of free babysitting for a new hairstyle? Or maybe you need some typing done. Or a dress altered. Or piano lessons. You may even find a dentist who will do a free exam in exchange for some free babysitting. The possibilities are endless. Discuss this idea with your co-op and find out what talents are available. Rates of exchange should be determined by the people involved.

When a *new baby* is born to a member it would be an appropriate time to have a get-together and present the mother with a gift of babysitting hours from her fellow co-op members. Each member could contribute as she wishes or a set number of hours could be given by each member. What gift would be more appreciated by a co-op mother than some relief time from her new baby? Because return sitting may be difficult when there is a new baby in the family, this gift will be especially appreciated because it will allow her to gad a bit without being concerned about her debit mounting at a time when she may not feel up to doing any sitting in return.

You may want to arrange an ongoing *sewing circle* with interested members. This could be combined with a topic of mutual interest for discussion, such as comparing nursery schools, toilet training, a book, local elections, etc.

If your co-op gets really organized and wants to do some *fund-raising,* a *baby equipment rental service* might be a good money-maker. And think of the great "hand-me-down" toy and childrens' clothing *rummage sales* that you could stage. Not to mention the money-saving trading you can do right within your own co-op.

HAVE FUN!

*Pot-luck dinners and picnics will tend to be
the most common type of co-op get-together.*

FEEDBACK

Please help to make the next edition of this book even more useful. Write to us with your suggestions for improving the information contained in this book. Specifically let us hear from you about alternative methods of bookkeeping and any unmentioned rules you feel should be included, along with an explanation as to why.

Send your comments to:

Carousel Press
P.O. Box 6061
Albany, CA   94706.

- -

ORDER FORM

Make checks payable to *Carousel Press* and mail to:

Carousel Press, P.O. Box 6061, Albany, CA 94706

_____ *How to Organize a Babysitting Cooperative,* hardcover @ $8.95 each . . . $_____

_____ *How to Organize a Babysitting Cooperative,* soft cover @ $3.95 each . . . $_____

_____ *Eating Out With the Kids in San Francisco and the Bay Area* @ $3.45 ea. $_____

_____ *Weekend Adventures for City-Weary Families* @ $3.95 each . . . . $_____

<table>
<tr><td></td><td align="right">subtotal</td><td>$_____</td></tr>
<tr><td>☐ Please send fund-raising brochure.</td><td align="right">6½% sales tax (Calif. residents only)</td><td>$_____</td></tr>
<tr><td>☐ Please send retailer's brochure.</td><td align="right">postage/handing</td><td>$_____ .50</td></tr>
<tr><td></td><td align="right">total amount enclosed</td><td>$_____</td></tr>
</table>

SEND TO (please print):

name _____ phone _____

address _____

city, state, zip_____

ALL ORDERS MUST BE PREPAID. Make check or money order payable to CAROUSEL PRESS and mail to:

CAROUSEL PRESS, P.O. Box 6061, Albany, CA 94706

VISITING   CALIFORNIA ?

EATING OUT? TAKING THE KIDS ALONG?

This unique guide helps make dining out as a family an enjoyable experience. It allows parents to choose restaurants which are equipped to accommodate their children.
Parents will not find the usual hamburger, taco, and pizza chains listed. Instead they will find a variety of more unusual restaurants—all amenable to families. Each restaurant's description specifies the availability of highchairs and booster seats, average waiting time, and parking facilities—plus other important dining information.

Eating Out with the Kids in San Francisco and the Bay Area

CAROLE TERWILLIGER MEYERS

WANT TO GET AWAY FROM IT ALL?

Overnight trips will become more fun to plan and experience with the aid of this new guide for families. Practical suggestions for planning trips and traveling with children preface this book. Packed with information on interesting and fun places for families to visit, detailed trips include Santa Cruz, the Monterey Peninsula, Big Sur, San Simeon, Morro Bay, Mendocino, Eureka, the Wine Country, the Russian River, Lake Tahoe, the Gold Rush Country, and Yosemite. Each destination includes information on where to stay, where to eat, and what to do as well as such helpful extras as available babysitting, driving route, where to stop along the way, and where to write for further information. With this book in your library you will never be at a loss as to where to go to "get away from it all."

Weekend Adventures for City-Weary Families
A Guide to Overnight Trips in Northern California

Carole Terwilliger Meyers

Photo by Stephen Kane

ABOUT THE AUTHOR

Carole Terwilliger Meyers attended UCLA where she was a member of several student residence cooperatives. After graduating from San Francisco State College with a degree in Anthropology, she went on to earn a teaching credential from Fresno State College. She then taught elementary school for three years in the San Francisco Bay Area. Supportive of the cooperative way, Ms. Meyers is presently a member of a grocery store cooperative, is a charter member of a babysitting cooperative, and her son attends a parent-participation cooperative nursery school. Currently she resides in Berkeley, California where she acts as editor for the San Francisco Bay Area ASPO (American Society for Psychoprophylaxis in Obstetrics) Newsletter, devoted to the Lamaze method of prepared childbirth, and teaches a crochet class in Adult School. This is her second book. Her first was co-authored and entitled *Eating Out With the Kids in the East Bay.*